Contents

Introduction

Wood decks can be great things. They give you a place to relax and entertain outside, while maintaining one of the big advantages of staying in: a flat stable floor. In the last 30 years, decks have overtaken the old fashioned patio. One reason for this is that decks are made of wood, not masonry, so the design possibilities are almost limitless. Wood decks do wear out and must be maintained to last a long time and look good while doing it.

In addition to maintenance, once your deck has been built, you may decide it needs occasional updates. What about some lighting? Low voltage options are available that can really lighten up your deck. In-step lights and rope lighting on the railings not only extend the hours of use for your deck, they also improve safety.

Why have just any old wooden railing when you can expand your view with either a glass or cable system? Either is easy to install and can also serve to modernize the look of your favorite hangout.

Have a second story deck and don't find the space underneath to be particularly usable? Adding an underdeck enclosure with gutters will keep the area under your deck clean and dry. The newly protected area can become additional outdoor space in the form of a patio, or could serve as protected space for storage of garden or play equipment.

Finally, a few planter boxes can help add greenery and color to your deck.

Project: Maintain & Renew a Deck

Weathered wood has true romantic appeal, but when the wood is the only thing between your feet and the ground it ought to be in pristine shape. Refinishing a wood deck is vital to that cause (and you'll need to learn how, since you'll be doing it practically every year).

If you have a small deck (anything under 200 sq. ft.), refinishing is a pretty easy job. But on larger decks, refinishing can develop into quite a chore. The thing to remember, when you've been scrubbing off the old finish for hours, is that replacing a deck can eat up $10,000 in a heartbeat. So it pays to take care of problems before deck damage gets out of control.

Inspect your deck once each year. Replace loose or rusting hardware or fasteners, and apply fresh finish to prevent water damage. Look carefully for areas that show signs of damage. Replace or reinforce damaged wood as soon as possible. Restore an older, weathered deck to the original wood color with a deck-brightening solution. Brighteners are available at any home improvement store.

> **TIP:** Inspect hidden areas regularly for signs of rotted or damaged wood. Apply a fresh coat of finish yearly.

Refinishing a deck involves three separate steps. The first is to remove the old finish. The second is to wash away all the dirt, mildew, and other residues. And the third is to reseal the surface with a new finish. There are lots of products on the market for cleaning decks. The trick is to get the product that's right for your situation. Anything that just says "deck cleaner" is not what's needed. These help lift off dirt and grime but won't do much to remove an old finish. If your deck is covered with just a transparent sealer or a light stain, then a product called a "stain/sealer remover" is what you need. If you have a heavy, solid-color stain, you'll want something stronger. These are sometimes called simply "deck finish strippers," and are made to lift off everything from the surface.

> **TIP:** Use an awl or screwdriver to check deck for soft, rotted wood.

Replace or reinforce damaged wood. Clean debris from cracks between decking boards with a putty knife. Debris traps moisture, and can cause wood to rot.

Tools & Materials

- Deck brightener
- Deck stripper
- Stiff bristle brush
- Deck sprayer
- Bucket
- Masking tape
- Plastic sheeting or butcher paper
- Paint brush and roller
- Sealant or stain

How to Renew an Unfinished Deck

1. Drive new fasteners to secure loose decking to joists. If using the old nail or screw holes, new fasteners should be slightly longer than the originals.

2. Mix deck-brightening solution as directed by manufacturer. Apply solution with pressure sprayer. Let solution set for 10 minutes.

3. Scrub deck thoroughly with a stiff scrub brush. Wear rubber gloves and eye protection.

4. Rinse deck with clear water. If necessary, apply a second coat of brightener to extremely dirty or stained areas. Rinse and let dry. Apply a coat of sealer or stain.

How To Renew a Finished Deck

1. Apply a heavy coat of deck stripper to the deck boards. Usually a garden sprayer works for this job. But you can also use a paint roller with a long nap roller to spread the stripper.

2. Let the stripper set for as long as the container directions recommend (usually around 15 minutes). Then brush it vigorously with a stiff bristle deck brush. Try to avoid splattering the stripper on nearby plants, the siding, trim or windows and doors.

3. Rinse off the stripper using a garden hose with a spray attachment or use a pressure washer. Be sure to rinse any adjacent surfaces that might have been splattered with stripper.

4. Next comes the deck cleaner, which is often sold in a concentrated form. Mix it thoroughly in a large bucket, according to the container's directions.

5. Using a stiff deck brush, spread the deck cleaner over the boards and scrub until the wood brightens. Usually, this happens almost immediately. Keep scrubbing until the surface looks new.

6. Protect surrounding surfaces with masking tape and paper, then start brushing on the sealer. Use the brush just for hard to reach areas. Use a roller on everything else.

7. Apply sealer to the open areas with a roller that has a 3/4"-nap roller cover. As you move, press the roller down forcefully so the sealer squeezes between the boards and covers their edges.

TIP: Keep in mind, when working with the brush, that it tends to hold less sealer than a paint roller. So, to ensure even coverage, load up the brush with extra sealer and apply it in a heavier coat.

Repairing a Deck

Replace or reinforce damaged deck wood as soon as possible. Wood rot can spread and weaken solid wood.

After replacing or reinforcing the rotted wood, clean the entire deck and apply a fresh coat of clear sealer-preservative or staining sealer. Apply a fresh coat of finish each year to prevent future water damage. If you need to repair more than a few small areas, it is probably time to replace the entire deck.

Tools & Materials

- Cat's paw or flat pry bar
- Screwgun
- Awl or screwdriver
- Hammer
- Chisel
- Eye protection
- Pressure-sprayer
- Circular saw
- Scrub brush
- Paint brush
- Drill or hammer drill
- 5/8" masonry bit
- Level
- Ratchet wrench
- Sealer-preservative or staining sealer
- Galvanized nails (6d, 10d)
- Deck lumber
- Baking soda
- Corrosion-resistant deck screws
- Rubber gloves

- Bucket

How to Repair Damaged Decking & Joists

1. Remove nails or screws from the damaged decking board, using a cat's paw or screwgun. Remove the damaged board.

2. Inspect the underlying joists for signs of rotted wood. Joists with discolored, soft areas should be repaired and reinforced.

3. Use a hammer and chisel to remove any rotted portions of joist.

4. Apply a thick coat of sealer-preservative to damaged joist. Let dry, then apply a second coat of sealer. Cut a reinforcing joist (sister joist) from pressure-treated lumber.

5. Treat all sides of sister joist with clear sealer-preservative, and let dry. Position sister joist tightly against the damaged joist, and attach with 10d nails driven every 2 feet.

6. Attach sister joist to ledger and header joist by toenailing with 10d nails. Cut replacement decking boards from matching lumber, using a circular saw.

7. If the existing decking is gray, "weather" the new decking by scrubbing with a solution made from 1 cup baking soda and 1 gallon warm water. Rinse and let dry.

Project: Glass-Panel Railing

For the ultimate in unobstructed viewing, you can install a glass-panel railing system on your deck and avoid balusters altogether. The system shown here is quite manageable to install without special tools. It consists of a framework of aluminum posts and top and bottom rails that fasten together with screws. Extruded vinyl liner inserts that fit inside the top and bottom rails hold the glass without fasteners. Tempered glass panels that are at least 1/4" thick will meet building codes, provided the railing posts are spaced five feet on center. It is recommended that you assemble the railing framework first, then measure and order the glass panels to fit the rail openings.

Tools & Materials

- Tape measure
- Level
- Ratchet and sockets or impact driver
- Drill/driver
- Posts
- Post brackets

- Tempered glass panels
- Fasteners
- Railings
- Lag screws
- Attachment screws
- Rubber setting blocks

How To Install a Glass-Panel Railing

1. Once you've determined the layout of the deck posts, fasten the post brackets to the deck with lag screws. Install all the posts and bottom rails.

2. Insert the top post sleeves into the post ends, then measure and cut the top rails to length. Assemble the rails and sleeves, fastening the parts with screws. Check each post for plumb with a level before driving the attachment screws and adjust if necessary.

3. Measure the length of the top rail inner channels and cut glass insert strips to fit. Fasten the glass rail brackets to the posts with screws.

4. Measure the distance between the glass inserts and add 3/4" to determine the height of the glass panels. Measure the distance between posts and subtract 3 to 6" to find the glass panel width, less air gaps. Order glass. Install the bottom rails on the brackets.

5. Slip each glass panel into the top insert, swing it into place over the bottom insert, and lower it into the bottom channel to rest on the rubber setting blocks. No further attachment is required.

Project: Steel Cable Railing

Another railing option that can improve the view from your deck is braided steel cables between the railing posts. Here, lengths of cable pass continuously through holes in the posts and tension is created with a special threaded fitting on the cable end. Cables must be spaced no more than 3" apart, with railing posts located 3 ft. on center. You can buy prefabricated metal posts as we show here or make them from wood. The endmost posts should be made of 4 × 6 lumber to handle the cable tension, although the intermediate posts can be conventionally sized. You'll also need to install a 2 × 6 cap rail securely to all posts and add 1 × 4 blocking under the cap rail to provide additional lateral reinforcement.

TIP: A series of braided steel cables can replace ordinary wood balusters and give your deck a clean, contemporary look. Posts must be spaced closely together to handle the cable tension and ensure safety.

Tools & Materials

- Measuring tape

- Level
- Drill/driver
- Hack saw
- Cable cutters
- Self-locking pliers
- Wrenches
- Electric grinder
- Cable-lacing needle
- Cap rails
- Steel lag screws & washers
- Self-locking fitting
- Cable
- Flanged metal posts

How To Install Cable Railings

1. If you install flanged metal posts, secure them to the deck's framing with stainless steel lag screws and washers.

2. Drill holes through the railing posts to fit the cables, threaded end fittings, and quick connect locking fittings. Pass the terminal threaded ends of the cables through one railing end post and install washer nuts about 1/4" onto the threads.

3. Feed the cables through the intermediate posts and the opposite end post. Work systematically to prevent tangling the cables. A cable-lacing needle will make it easier to pass cables through each post without snagging it. Attach cap rails.

4. Slip a self-locking fitting over the end of each cable and seat the fitting in the cable hole in the post. You may need to counterbore this hole first to accommodate the fitting. Pull the cable tight. Jaws inside the fitting will prevent the cable from becoming slack again.

5. Tighten each cable nut with a wrench, starting from the center cable and working outward. A locking pliers will keep the cable from twisting as you tighten the nut. Tighten the nut until you cannot flex the cables more than 4" apart.

6. Cut off the excess cable at the quick-connect fitting end with a cable cutter or hack saw. Grind the end of the cable flush with the fitting, and cover it with a snap-on end cap.

Project: Low-Voltage Step Lights

Low-voltage recessed lights are great for decks. Installed inconspicuously in the deck boards, they provide accent lighting for plant boxes or pathway lighting for stairs.

Tools & Materials

- Jigsaw
- Drill and bits
- Measuring tape
- Low-voltage step light
- Combination tool
- Wire connectors
- Low-voltage cable and transformer

How to Install Low-Voltage Step Lights

1. Use the template or trace the bottom of the fixture onto the treads to mark a hole for each light. Center the fixture on the tread, 1 to 2" from the edge (the hole will center on the gap between the 2 × 6s on most deck stairs). Drill holes at the corners, then cut the holes with a jigsaw. Test the fixtures to be sure they will fit (they should fit snugly), and adjust the holes as necessary.

2. Run cable to the stairs from an existing low-voltage system or from a new transformer. Drill a hole in the bottom riser if necessary, and snake the cable under the stairs along the inside edge. Pull a loop of cable through each of the holes for the fixtures and temporarily secure it to the tread with tape.

3. At the middle of the first loop of cable in the series, separate 3 to 4" of the two conductors in the cable by slicing down the center. Strip about 2" of insulation off of each wire. Cut the wire in the center of the stripped section, and twist the two ends and the end of one of the fixture wires into an outdoor wire connector. Secure the connection with electrical tape. Repeat with the other fixture wire and the other circuit wire. Tuck the wires back into the hole, and place the fixture into the hole. Test each fixture before installing the next one.

Project: Low-Voltage Railing Lights

Rope light is thin, flexible, clear tubing with tiny light bulbs embedded every few inches along its length. Most rope lights are meant to plug into a receptacle and use household current. While this is all right for indoor decorating, it limits their use outdoors. Low voltage versions, however, are powered by transformers and can be connected inconspicuously to a low voltage landscape lighting circuit. They are available from specialty lighting stores and catalogs.

Tools & Materials

- Low-voltage cable
- Cable staples
- Rope light
- Combination tool
- U-channel
- Hammer
- Nails

How to Install Low-Voltage Railing Lights

1. Run a cable from a transformer or from a nearby low voltage circuit using a T-connector. Route the cable up a post at the end of the rail, and secure it with cable staples. Leave enough length at the end of the cable to connect it to the rope light.

2. Secure the rope light to the underside of the railing with U-channel. Cut the channel to length, and nail it to the bottom of the railing. Press the rope into the channel.

3. Connect the fixture cord to the end of the rope with the twist-on fitting. Connect the rope wires to the branch cable with a cable connector designed for low-voltage outdoor cable. Cap the end of the rope with a plastic cap.

Project: Under-Deck Enclosure

Second-story walkout decks can be a mixed blessing. On top, you have an open, sun-filled perch with a commanding view of the landscape. The space below the deck, however, is all too often a dark and chilly nook that is functionally unprotected from water runoff. As a result, an under-deck area often ends up as wasted space or becomes a holding area for seasonal storage items or the less desirable outdoor furniture. But there's an easy way to reclaim all that convenient outdoor space—by installing a weatherizing ceiling system that captures runoff water from the deck above, leaving the area below dry enough to convert into a versatile outdoor room. You can even enclose the space to create a screened in patio room. The under-deck system featured in this project is designed for do-it-yourself installation. Its components are made to fit almost any standard deck and come in three sizes to accommodate different deck-joist spacing (for 12", 16", and 24" on-center spacing). Once the system is in place, you can begin adding amenities like overhead lighting, ceiling fans, and speakers to complete the outdoor room environment.

The system works by capturing water that falls through the decking above and channeling it to the outside edge of the deck. Depending on your plans, you can let the water fall from the ceiling panels along the deck's edge, or you can install a standard rain gutter and downspout to direct the water to a single exit point on the ground or a rain barrel. Steps for adding a gutter system are also included.

This under-deck system consists of four main parts: The joist rails mount to the deck joists and help secure the other components. The collector panels span the joist cavity to capture water falling through the deck above. Water flows to the sides of the panels where it falls through gaps in the joist rails and into the joist gutters (for interior joists) and boundary gutters (for outer joists). The gutters carry the water to the outside edge of the deck.

TIP: For a finished look, paint the decking lumber that will be exposed after the system is installed. Typically, the lower portion of the ledger board (attached to the house) and the outer rim joist (at the outer edge of the deck) remain exposed.

Tools & Materials

- 4-ft. level
- Chalk line
- Caulking gun
- Drill
- Aviation snips
- Under-deck ceiling system
- Waterproof acrylic caulk
- 1" stainless steel screws

- Hacksaw (for optional rain gutter)
- Rain gutter system (optional)

How to Install an Under-Deck System

1. Check the undersides of several deck joists to make sure the structure is level. This is important for establishing the proper slope for effective water flow.

2. If your deck is not level, you must compensate for this when setting the ceiling slope. To determine the amount of correction that's needed, hold one end of the level against a joist and tilt the level until it reads perfectly level. Measure the distance from the joist to the free end of the level. Then, divide this measurement by the length of the level. For example, if the distance is 1/4" and the level is 4 ft. long, the deck is out of level by 1/16" per foot.

3. To establish the slope for the ceiling system, mark the ends of the joists closest to the house: Measure up from the bottom 1" for every 10 ft. of joist length (or approximately 1/8" per ft.) and make a mark. Mark both sides of each intermediate joist and the inside faces of the outer joists.

4. Create each slope reference line using a chalk line: Hold one end of the chalk line at the mark made in Step 3, and hold the other end at the bottom edge of the joist where it meets the rim joist at the outside edge of the deck. Snap a reference line on all of the joists.

5. Install vinyl flashing along the ledger board in the joist cavities. Attach the flashing with 1" stainless steel screws. Caulk along the top edges of the flashing where it meets the ledger and both joists, using quality, waterproof acrylic caulk. Also caulk the underside of the flashing for an extra layer of protection.

6. Begin installing the joist rails, starting 1" away from the ledger. Position each rail with its bottom edge on the chalk line and fasten it to the joist at both ends with 1" stainless steel screws, then add one or two screws in between. Avoid over driving the screws and deforming the rail; leaving a little room for movement is best.

7. Install the remaining rails on each joist face, leaving a 1-1/2" (minimum) to 2" (maximum) gap between rails. Install rails along both sides of each interior joist and along the insides of each outside joist. Trim the final rail in each row as needed, using aviation snips.

8. Measure the full length of each joist cavity, and cut a collector panel 1/4" shorter than the cavity. This allows room for expansion of the panels. For narrower joist cavities, trim the panel to width following the manufacturer's sizing recommendations.

9. Scribe and trim collector panels for a tight fit against the ledger board. Hold a carpenter's pencil flat against the ledger, and move the pencil along the board to transfer its contours to the panel. Trim the panel along the scribed line.

10. Trim the corners of collector panels as needed to accommodate joist hangers and other hardware. This may be necessary only at the house side of the joist cavity; at the outer end, the 1/4" expansion gap should clear any hardware.

11. Install the collector panels, starting at the house. With the textured side of the panel facing down, insert one side edge into the joist rails, and then push up gently on the opposite side until it fits into the opposing rails. When fully installed, the panels should be tight against the ledger and have a 1/4" gap at the rim joist.

12. Prepare each joist gutter by cutting it 1/4" shorter than the joist it will attach to. On the house end of each gutter, trim the corners of the flanges at 45°. This helps the gutter fit tightly to the ledger.

13. Cut four or five 1/8" tabs into the bottom surface at the outside ends of the gutters. This helps promote the drainage of water over the edge of the gutter.

14. Attach self-adhesive foam weatherstrip (available from the manufacturer) at the home-end of each joist gutter. Run a bead of caulk along the foam strip to water-seal it to the gutter. The weatherstrip serves as a water dam.

15. Install each joist gutter by spreading its sides open slightly while pushing the gutter up onto the joist rails until it snaps into place. The gutter should fit snugly against the collector panels. The gutter's home-end should be tight against the ledger, with the 1/4" expansion gap at the rim joist.

16. Prepare the boundary gutters following the same steps used for the joist gutters. Install each boundary gutter by slipping its long, outside flange behind the joist rails and pushing up until the gutter snaps into place. Install the boundary gutters working from the house side to the outer edge of the deck.

17. Run a bead of color-matched caulk along the joint where the collector panels meet the ledger board. This is for decorative purposes only and is not required to prevent water intrusion.

18. If collector panels are misshapen because the joist spacing is too tight, free the panel within the problem area, then trim about 1/8" from the side edge of the panel. Reset the panel in the rails. If necessary, trim the panel edge again in slight increments until the panel fits properly.

Under-Deck Runoff Gutters

A basic gutter system for a square or rectangular deck includes a straight run of gutter channel with a downspout at one end. Prefabricated vinyl or aluminum gutter parts are ideal for this application. Gutter channels are commonly available in 10-ft. and 20-ft. lengths, so you might be able to use a single channel without seams. Otherwise, you can join sections of channel with special connectors. Shop around for the best type of hanger for your situation. If there's limited backing to support the back side of the channel or to fasten into, you may have to use strap type hangers that can be secured to framing above the gutter.

TIP: Gutters come in several material types, including PVC, enameled steel, and copper. In most cases you should try and match the surrounding trim materials, but using a more decorative material for contrast can be effective.

Tools & Materials
- 4-ft. level
- Chalk line
- Drill
- Aviation snips
- Hacksaw
- Rain gutter system

How to Install an Under-Deck Runoff Gutter

1. Snap a chalk line onto the beam or other supporting surface to establish the slope of the main gutter run. The line will correspond to the top edge of the gutter channel. The ideal slope is 1/16" per foot. For example, with a 16-ft.-long gutter, the beginning is 1" higher than the end. The downspout should be located just inside the low end of the gutter channel. Mark the beam at both ends to create the desired slope, then snap a chalk line between the marks. The high end of the gutter should be just below the boundary gutter in the ceiling system.

2. Install a downspout outlet near the end of the gutter run so the top of the gutter is flush with the slope line. If you plan to enclose the area under the deck, choose an inconspicuous location for the downspout, away from traffic areas.

3. Install hanger clips (depending on the type of hangers or support clips you use, it is often best to install them before installing the gutter channel). Attach a hanger every 24" so the top of the gutter will hang flush with slope line.

4. Cut sections of gutter channel to size using a hacksaw. Attach an end cap to the beginning of the main run, then fit the channel into the downspout outlet (allowing for expansion, if necessary) and secure the gutter in place.

5. Join sections of channel together, if necessary, using connectors. Install a short section of channel with an end cap on the opposite side of the downspout outlet. Paint the area where the downspout will be installed if it is unpainted.

6. Cut the downspout piping to length and fasten an elbow fitting to its bottom end. Attach the downspout to the downspout outlet, then secure the downspout to a post or other vertical support using hangers.

7. Cut a drain pipe to run from the downspout elbow to a convenient drainage point. Position the pipe so it directs water away from the house and any traffic areas. Attach the pipe to the downspout elbow. Add a splash block, if desired.

> **TIP:** You may have to get a little creative when routing the downspout drain in an enclosed porch or patio.

Project: Planter Boxes

Decorating a deck is much like decorating a room in your home—it's nice to have pieces that are adaptable enough that you can move them around occasionally and create a completely new look. After all, most of us can't buy new furniture every time we get tired of the way our living rooms look. And we can't build or buy new deck furnishings every time we want to rearrange the deck.

That's one of the reasons this trio of planter boxes works so well. In addition to being handsome—especially when flowers are bursting out of them— they're incredibly adaptable. You can follow these plans to build a terrific trio of planter boxes that will go well with each other and will complement most decks. Or you can tailor the plans to suit your needs. For instance, you may want three boxes that are exactly the same size. Or you might want to build several more and use them as a border that encloses a patio or frames a terraced area.

Whatever the dimensions of the boxes, the basic construction steps are the same. If you decide to alter the designs, take a little time to figure out the new dimensions and sketch plans. Then devise a new cutting list and do some planning so you can make efficient use of materials. To save cutting time, clamp together parts that are the same size and shape and cut them as a group (called gang cutting).

When your planter boxes have worn out their welcome in one spot, you can easily move them to another, perhaps with a fresh coat of stain, and add new plantings. You can even use the taller boxes to showcase outdoor relief sculptures—a kind of alfresco sculpture gallery.

Whether you build only one or all three, these handy cedar planters are small enough to move around your gardens and inside your greenhouse or garden shed.

Tools & Materials

- Tape measure
- Miter box and backsaw
- 1-1/4" galvanized deck screws
- Landscape fabric
- Circular saw
- (3) 8-ft. cedar 1 × 2s
- 1-5/8" galvanized deck screws
- Straightedge
- (6) 8-ft. cedar 1 × 4s
- 6d galvanized finish nails
- Drill
- 4 × 8-ft. sheet of 5/8" T1-11 siding
- Exterior wood stain
- Finishing sander
- 2 × 4-ft. piece 3/4" CDX plywood
- Paintbrush

Cutting List

2 End panels from siding:

- Box A: 5/8 × 15 × 11-1/8"
- Box B: 5/8 × 15 × 17-1/8"
- Box C: 5/8 × 15 × 23-1/8"

2 Side panels from siding:

- Box A: 5/8 × 22-1/4 × 11-1/8"
- Box B: 5/8 × 10-1/4 × 17-1/8"
- Box C: 5/8 × 10-1/4 × 23-1/8"

8 Corner trim from cedar:

- Box A: 7/8 × 3-1/2 × 11-1/8"
- Box B 7/8 × 3-1/2 × 17-1/8"
- Box C: 7/8 × 3-1/2 × 23-1/8"

2 Bottom trim from cedar:

- Box A: 7/8 × 3-1/2 × 9-1/4"
- Box B 7/8 × 3-1/2 × 9-1/4"
- Box C: 7/8 × 3-1/2 × 9-1/4"

2 Bottom trim from cedar:

- Box A: 7/8 × 3-1/2 × 17"
- Box B 7/8 × 3-1/2 × 5"
- Box C: 7/8 × 3-1/2 × 5"

2 Top caps from cedar:

- Box A: 7/8 × 1-1/2 × 18"
- Box B 7/8 × 1-1/2 × 18"
- Box C: 7/8 × 1-1/2 × 18"

2 Top caps from cedar:

- Box A: 7/8 × 1-1/2 × 24"
- Box B 7/8 × 1-1/2 × 12"

• Box C: 7/8 × 1-1/2 × 12"

1 Bottom panel from plywood:

• Box A: 3/4 × 14-1/2 × 19-1/2"

• Box B 3/4 × 14-1/2 × 8-1/2"

• Box C: 3/4 × 14-1/2 × 8-1/2"

2 Cleats from cedar:

• Box A: 7/8 × 1-1/2 × 12"

• Box B 7/8 × 1-1/2 × 12"

• Box C: 7/8 × 1-1/2 × 12"

• Note: Measurements reflect the actual size of dimension lumber.

How to Build Planter Boxes

1. Cut all the wood parts to size according to the Cutting List. Use a circular saw and a straightedge cutting guide to rip siding panels. You can make all three sizes, or any combination you choose.

2. Assemble the box frame. Place the end panel face down and butt it against a side panel. Mark the locations of several fasteners on the side panel. Drill counterbored 3/32" pilot holes in the side panel at the marked locations and fasten the side panel to the end panel with 1-5/8" deck screws. Fasten the opposite side panel the same way. Attach the other end panel with deck screws.

3. Attach the corner trim. Position one piece of corner trim flush to the corner edge and fasten to the panels with 1-5/8" galvanized deck screws driven into the trim from the inside of the box. Place the second piece of trim flush to the edge of the first piece, creating a square butt joint. Attach to the panel with 1-5/8" galvanized deck screws. For extra support, end nail the two trim pieces together at the corner with galvanized finish nails.

4. Attach the bottom trim. Fasten the bottom trim to the end and side panels, between the corner trim pieces and flush with the bottom of the box. Drive 1-1/4" deck screws through the panels from the inside to fasten the trim pieces to the box.

5. Attach the cap pieces. Cut 45° miters at both ends of one cap piece using a miter box and backsaw or a power miter saw. Tack this piece to the top end of the box, with the outside edges flush with the outer edges of the corner trim. Miter both ends of each piece and tack to the box to make a square corner with the previously installed piece. Once all caps are tacked in position and the miters are closed cleanly, attach the cap pieces using 6d galvanized finish nails.

6. Install the cleats to hold the box bottom in place. Screw to the inside of the end panels with 1-5/8" deck screws. If your planter is extremely tall, fasten the cleats higher on the panels so you won't need as much soil to fill the box. If doing so, add cleats on the side panels as well for extra support.

7. Finish and install the bottom. Cut the bottom panel to size from 3/4"-thick exterior-rated plywood. Drill several 1"-dia. drainage holes in the panel and set it onto the cleats. The bottom panel does not need to be fastened in place, but for extra strength, nail it to the cleats and box sides with galvanized finish nails.

8. Finish the box or boxes with wood sealer-preservative. When the finish has dried, line the planter box with landscape fabric, stapling it at the top of the box. Trim off fabric at least a couple of inches below the top of the box. Add a 2"-layer of gravel or stones, then fill with a 50/50 mix of potting soil and compost.

TIP: Add wheels or casters to your planter boxes before filling them with soil. Be sure to use locking wheels or casters with brass or plastic housings.

For safety, use caution, care, and good judgment when following the procedures described in this book. The Publisher cannot assume responsibility for any damage to property or injury to persons as a result of misuse of the information provided.

The techniques shown in this book are general techniques for various applications. In some instances, additional techniques not shown in this book may be required. Always follow manufacturers' instructions included with products, since deviating from the directions may void warranties. The projects in this book vary widely as to skill levels required: some may not be appropriate for all do-it-yourselfers, and some may require professional help. Consult your local Building Department for information on building permits, codes, and other laws as they apply to your project.